Spiralizer Cookbook

Low Carb, Gluten-Free, Grain-Free Recipes for Your Favorite Noodles, Pastas, Soups, Salads with a Healthy Approach

2

Copyright Notice

Disclaimer

3

Table of Contents

Foreword

"I wouldn't exactly call it 'cooking' but I can make noodles. That means I can boil water, put the pasta in and wait until it's done."

- Devon Werkheiser

I have a spiralizer in my kitchen and for the longest time, I used it very rarely, on occasions when I wanted something to look fancy for a dinner party. I didn't realize until recently that this is one of the best kitchen appliances you can have.

I'm not very handy with knives, I will admit. Trying to cut something into spirals with a knife is not only inconceivable for me, but probably pretty dangerous, too. I'd like to keep all my fingers! So, the spiralizer is an absolute must for me, if I plan to make spiralized recipes and stick to the diet plan I've set up for myself. Fortunately, the food I can make with it is so delicious and healthy, everyone in my family can enjoy it, even the little ones.

You'll love these recipes, made with this incredibly cool appliance. Maintaining a diet that is gluten and grain free might sound intimidating but with a spiralizer, using substitutions for typical noodles is so much easier. How can this be? You might be asking. The answer is simple. You can use nearly any vegetable or fruit and turn it into a noodle instead. Apples, as you will see from the recipes in this book, are an excellent substitute and they taste delicious. You will also notice that zucchini noodles, which contain neither gluten or grain, are another wonderful substitute for traditional noodles. They tend to be very watery so you'll need to dry them when you use them or they can make your sauces also watery.

If you're cooking zucchini noodles, toss them in a pan and sauté them. You can also consider salting them, like you would do with eggplant (also a cool veggie to spiralize).

Here's a tip for you. It is possible to avoid creating half-moons with your veggies. If this starts happening, the vegetable has probably gone off center. Reposition the vegetable so that the blade is centered. Flip the veggie around and center the other end to get it as cylindrical as possible.

Like zucchini, cucumbers are a very watery vegetable. It is also an ingredient that people love to spiralize. Keep in mind that they are made of over 95% water. You will definitely need to pat it dry with a paper towel. Probably more than one! Lay the cucumber noodles on two layers of paper towels. Cover with two more. Lean on the cucumbers to absorb all the moisture. You may even have to do this twice. Always do this gently so that the noodles aren't ruined.

I hope you enjoy the recipes we've selected for this book. Try each one and pick your favorite. We had a lot of fun with our spiralizer and we hope you will, too!

Bonus: Your FREE Gift

As a token of our appreciation, please take advantage of the **FREE Gift** - a lifetime **VIP Membership** at our book club.

Follow the link below to download your FREE books:

http://bit.ly/vipbookclub

As a VIP member, you will get an instant **FREE** access to exclusive new releases and bestselling books.

Chapter One: Introducing the Spiralized

Diet

"Eating healthy is a constant battle. I love chips. I'm a huge pasta fan."

- *Hayden Panetierre*

In this chapter, I will help you to:

- Cook with a spiralizer

- Learn the best substitutes, tips, and tricks to help maintain your diet plan

When you use a spiralizer, you open the doors to a new adventure in the kitchen. For many, this gadget is a dream-come-true. Your favorite vegetables and fruits suddenly become noodles and ribbons that you can use as substitutes for common, everyday prepackaged noodles. You wouldn't believe how much healthier using a spiralizer is. Your noodles can be razor-thin or thick enough to hold a sauce.

A lot of the time, people who own a spiralizer will not use it often. Many people are unaware how much healthier it is to use spiralized fruits and veggies rather than the regular noodles until they put themselves on a diet that requires special care with the meals they prepare. When you are on a low-carb, gluten, and grain-free diet, this is the time to break out the spiralizer and use it as often as possible. The end result is usually the same. The spiralizer continues to be used even after the diet has ended. It's just that good!

Simply put, a spiralizer is a tool used in the kitchen that has different blade settings and a pronged handle so that you can crank out vegetables and fruits in curly ribbons. These strands are then used to create meals that would otherwise have had traditional noodles in the recipe. You can get a spiralizer that is made of plastic. It is easy to maneuver and lightweight so that it's easy to use. The only problem with plastic spiralizers is that they tend to stain and can be somewhat hard to clean. You will choose what kind of spiralizer you want when you check them out at the department store.

Not sure how to use a spiralizer? It's very simple. You'll slide your blade attachment into the appliance and place the fruit in between the blades. Turn the handle so that the vegetable or fruit is pushed through the blades.

Here are a few of the most common fruits and veggies used in the spiralizer.

Zucchini

Apples

Potatoes

Cucumbers

Radishes

Beets

Sweet Potatoes

Pumpkin

Butternut squash

Carrots

Summer Squash

Restaurant chefs love this device. They have a lot more slicing and dicing and chopping to do than someone who cooks only for themselves or their family. They are also known to use a mandolin slicer, which you might have in your home, as well. They both work well, but a spiralizer produces prettier ribbons and noodles than a mandolin slicer. It is also a bit easier to use because you are cranking a handle instead of slicing in a horizontal motion repeatedly. Restaurant chefs tend to use this gadget more than any other slicer in their kitchens.

It really is easy to create pasta that is low-carb, gluten-free and grain-free without losing all of the flavorings that make you want to eat in the first place. When you start a diet where you don't eat grains, you will quickly realize the value of your spiralizer in creating healthier "pasta". Not only have chefs around the world created pasta noodles from vegetables and fruits, but they have also discovered a method for rice, as well. Simply pulverize the spiralized vegetables with a food processor and you've got the perfect "rice" for your meal.

In a culture where meat is a main food and vegetables come second, it is nice to discover you are getting more vegetables in your diet than you ever did before, without even realizing it or sacrificing taste and flavor.

An important thing to remember about using spiralized vegetables and fruit in place of grain pasta noodles is that they will not taste the same. When you think about it, pasta noodles by themselves don't taste like much either. It is the toppings you add that make the meal delicious. The sauces, seasonings, and meats provide flavor for otherwise bland tasting noodles. Whatever you use as your "noodle" base, it will probably be more flavorful than a bowl of egg or grain-

16

based noodles by themselves. Take this into account when you are deciding whether or not to adjust the recipe in any way.

One of the most popular vegetables that is used with a spiralizer is zucchini. Zucchini noodles are the easiest to pair up with other ingredients to create delicious sauces. They are not heavy on taste but add something more than a typical run of the mill noodle. They soak up dressings quite nicely. Zucchini noodles also look the most like spaghetti noodles, which is often comforting to those who are on a special diet and miss their pasta dishes.

Apples are at the top of the list for the fruit side of the deal. While zucchini tops at the most popular for vegetables, apples definitely take the award when it comes to fruit. While there are plenty of fruits that can be spiralized, the apple is the one most people prefer.

Apples make a great pairing for different types of salads. Other ingredients that make for a delicious salad include grated carrots, dried cranberries, and sunflower seeds. You won't be putting sunflower seeds through your spiralizer but adding them to salads gives them that extra crunch you will love.

Spiralizers are one of the less expensive kitchen tools. Obviously, the different varieties will be sold for different prices but you can usually get one of the most popular brands for around $39.95. That's excellent when you consider that you will probably be changing up your entire eating routine to match your gluten-free, grain-free, low-carb diet plan.

17

When it comes to the recipes provided in this book, you may find one or two recipes with slightly more carbs than you want in your diet. When this happens, make adjustments with the ingredients that will allow you to still create the fabulous dish without sacrificing your diet plan in the meantime.

You can guarantee that when you make spiralized vegetables and fruits, you are creating a kind of pasta or noodle that is grain-free, gluten-free, and low carb, if not carb-free, as well. Your noodles will always be this way. It is the other stuff you add that you must worry about. If you don't want to use something that is mentioned in the recipe, it is perfectly fine. Some people have severe allergies, always taking precautions whenever they cook something. Chances are, there is the perfect substitute available.

The best thing about using a spiralizer is that you will be eating more vegetables than you usually do. Your diet plan doesn't have to be bland and tasteless, just because you are going gluten and grain free and eating few of the bad carbs that you've been consuming most of your life. You don't always have to eat a salad (though they are very healthy). You are eating a meal that is just as healthy just by fixing pretty, colorful, flavorful noodles from vegetables with your spiralizer.

Good luck and enjoy the recipes!

Chapter Two: 10 Salads and Soups

"A Jewish woman had two chickens. One got sick, so the woman made chicken soup out of the other one to help the sick one get well."

- *Henny Youngman*

In this chapter, you will learn:

- Tips to making delicious salads on a special diet

- Soups that will make your mouth water

Greek Arugula Salad

Prep Time	15 mins

Cook Time	0 mins
Total Time	15 mins
Servings	4-6
Calories	109
Carbs	9.2g

Ingredients

- 2 medium cucumbers, spiralized and chopped
- 2 c chopped tomatoes
- 2 c baby arugula
- ½ c crumbled feta
- ½ c fresh parsley
- ½ halved red onion, thinly sliced

- ½ c halved, pitted olives

  For the Vinaigrette

- ¼ c evoo

- ½ tsp dried oregano

- ½ tsp honey

- Salt and pepper to taste

- 1 pressed garlic clove

Let's Cook:

1. Combine all of the ingredients in a large bowl after spiralizing the cucumbers and any other ingredients you want to spiralize.

2. Add the vinaigrette ingredients together and mix well.

3. Pour the vinaigrette over the salad and serve.

Extra Tip:

Most spiralized recipes are best served immediately at room temperature, since the ingredients are routinely raw.

Greek Salad

Prep Time	15 mins
Cook Time	0 mins
Total Time	15 mins
Servings	4-6
Calories	129
Carbs	10g

Ingredients:

- 1 large cucumber spiralized
- 1 large diced tomato

- ½ c canned, drained, and rinsed chickpeas

- 4 tsp balsamic vinegar

- 4 tsp evoo

- 4 tsp water

- ¼ c crumbled feta cheese

- 4 tsp spicy brown mustard

- Dash of black pepper

- ¾ tsp honey

- Basil for garnish

Let's Cook:

1. Combine the water, evoo, honey, mustard, black pepper, and balsamic vinegar in a container that has a lid.

2. Cover the container with a lid and shake well to combine.

3. Put the tomatoes, feta, cucumber, and chickpeas in a mixing bowl and stir to combine.

4. Pour on the dressing and toss to coat the entire salad.

5. Serve right away and enjoy!

Spiralized Vegetable Salad

Prep Time	15 mins
Cook Time	0 mins
Total Time	15 mins
Servings	4-6
Calories	117
Carbs	8.6g

Ingredients

- 2 broccoli stalks

- 1 medium beet

- ¼ cucumber

- 2 jumbo carrots

  Toppings

- Almonds or Walnuts

- Sunflowers or chia seeds

- Store bought salad dressing

Let's Cook:

1. Wash off your cucumber, carrots, and beet.

2. Remove the tops of the broccoli, set aside to snack on.

3. Remove the ends of the carrots to create a flat base on both ends. Cut off the tip where it is not as thick around and set aside for snacking.

4. Get out your spiralizer and use it on all of the vegetables, using the thinnest setting available.

5. Combine all ingredients in a bowl and top with nuts or seeds, as well as the dressing you have chosen (ranch tastes pretty good with this).

Cucumber Zucchini Salad

Prep Time	5 mins
Cook Time	0 mins
Total Time	5 mins
Servings	4
Calories	94
Carbs	7.1

Ingredients

- 1 medium cucumber

- 1 medium zucchini

- 2 c baby spinach leaves

- 1 c halved cherry tomatoes

- 2 tbsp. olive oil

- 1 tsp spicy brown mustard

- ½ tsp salt

- ¼ tsp pepper

- 2 tbsp. minced basil

- Juice from a lemon

Let's Cook:

1. Use a medium mixing bowl to combine the lemon juice with the pepper to create the lemon basil vinaigrette.

2. Trim the ends off the zucchini. Use a spiralizer to create long, wide ribbons. Do this also with the cucumber and place the results in the bottom of the bowl on top of the vinaigrette.

3. Check your seasonings and adjust them according to your tastes.

4. Serve immediately.

Zucchini Pasta Salad

Prep Time	15 mins
Cook Time	15 mins (fridge)
Total Time	30 mins
Servings	4
Calories	121
Carbs	10.7g

Ingredients

- 2 medium zucchinis

- 1 c quartered artichoke hearts, drained and patted dry

- ¾ c cubed salami

- 3 thick slices of mozzarella cheese

- 1/3 c quartered black olives

- 6 halved cherry tomatoes

- ½ small thinly-sliced red onion

  Dressing

- 1 tbsp. evoo

- 2 tbsp. lemon juice

- ¼ tsp dried basil

- ¼ tsp dried oregano

- 1 ½ tbsp. red wine vinegar

- 1/8 tsp red pepper flakes

- Pepper and salt to taste

Let's Cook:

1. Slice the zucchini and spiralize them using Blade b.

2. Put them in a large mixing bowl with the tomatoes, mozzarella, salami, black olives, red onion, and artichoke hearts.

3. Combine the ingredients for your dressing and mix them together well.

4. Pour the dressing over the pasta and toss to mix well. Refrigerate for 15 minutes (or longer for better flavor). The dressing will soften the zucchini.

5. Transfer to your serving bowl. Enjoy!

Extra Tip:

Use all symmetrical foods for your spiralizer. If you have a vegetable or fruit that is not quite symmetrical, trim it or cut it in half.

Carbonara

Prep Time	20 mins
Cook Time	0 mins
Total Time	20 mins
Servings	2
Calories	314
Carbs	8.2

Ingredients

- 2 eggs

- 2/3 c pecorino cheese

- 2 tbsp. olive oil

- 1 egg yolk

- 2 oz. cubed pancetta

- 1 large zucchini spiralized

- 2 tbsp. grated Parmigiano cheese

- 2 tsp ground black pepper

Let's Cook:

1. Whisk eggs and yolk in a bowl. Add the Pecorino cheese. Mix together well.

2. Heat olive oil in a large skillet over medium heat. Cook by stirring in pancetta until completely cooked through. Should not be crispy. It should take 2 to 3 minutes.

3. Use your spiralizer to create your zucchini noodles. Cook them and stir them until warm but not soft. Pancetta should be slightly crispy. It should take 3 to 5 minutes.

4. Remove the skillet from the heat.

5. Pour the egg mixture over the zucchini noodles and top with black pepper and Parmigiano cheese.

Zucchini Noodle Soup

Prep Time	15 mins
Cook Time	45 mins
Total Time	1 hour
Servings	4
Calories	290
Carbs	12g

Ingredients

- 2 diced celery ribs

- 2 minced garlic cloves

- ½ c diced red onion, heaped

- 1 large diced carrot

- 1 small pinch of red pepper flakes

- 3 tsp fresh oregano

- 3 tsp fresh thyme

- 2 bay leaves

- 2 c water

- 3 medium zucchinis

- 6 c chicken broth (low sodium is best)

- 4 bone in chicken thighs

Let's Cook:

1. Put a large soup pot on the stove over medium heat and put in your onions, garlic, red pepper flakes, celery, and carrots. Cook for 3 to 5 minutes. The onions should look translucent and the veggies will "sweat".

2. Add in thyme and oregano. Cook for another minute. Stir often.

3. Place the chicken and bay leaf in with the mixture and pour chicken broth and water over it. It should be covered completely. Let this come to a boil.

4. When it starts to boil lower the heat to simmer and cook for 30 minutes.

5. Take the chicken out after 30 minutes and shred it. Set this aside with any juices.

6. Put the bones back into the pot and simmer uncovered for another 10 minutes.

7. While the bones simmer, cut your zucchinis in half and spiralize them. Set them aside.

8. Remove the bones and bay leaves. Discard both. Add shredded chicken and zoodles back to the pot.

9. Cook for 5 minutes or to your preference. Serve warm.

Extra Tip:

Decide on the size of your veggies and fruits based on the size of your spiralizer. There are varying sizes but if you have one that is handheld, you will not want to choose veggies and fruits that will not fit.

Sweet Potato and Sausage Soup

Prep Time	10 mins
Cook Time	20 mins
Total Time	30 mins
Servings	6-8
Calories	175
Carbs	14.2g

Ingredients

- 1 tbsp. olive oil

- ½ tsp dried oregano

- 1 lb. fresh ground raw pork

- 1 tsp dried thyme

- 2 medium carrots

- ½ medium onion

- 3 garlic cloves

- 30 oz. canned crushed tomatoes

- 4 c spinach

- 1 medium sweet potato

- 6 c low-sodium chicken broth

- 1 c half n half

- Serve with

- 1 tbsp. fresh parsley

- ¼ c grated Parmesan cheese

Let's Cook:

1. Chop up your carrots and onion. Mince the garlic and spiralize the sweet potato.

2. Cook the sausage in a skillet until it is done all the way through. Set this aside on a plate lined with paper towels.

3. Use a large pot to combine the spices, onion, and olive oil. Cook over medium heat. Sauté the onions until they are translucent. Add garlic and carrots. Sauté for 3 minutes.

4. Add the crushed tomatoes, cooked sausage, and chicken broth. Bring this to a boil. Simmer for 5 minutes.

5. Add spiralized sweet potatoes. Cook for 3 minutes. All vegetables should be softened. Add in the spinach. When it is wilted, add the half n half.

6. Bring the soup to a boil to heat all the way through. Remove from heat.

7. Serve with parmesan and parsley to garnish.

Ginger Scallion and Egg Drop Zucchini Noodles

Prep Time	10 mins
Cook Time	15 mins
Total Time	25 mins
Servings	2-4
Calories	211
Carbs	9.8g

Ingredients

- ¾ tbsp. evoo

- ½ lg zucchini

- 3 tbsp. dried seaweed

- ½ c chopped scallions

- 1 tbsp. minced ginger

- 2 tsp sherry vinegar

- 1 large beaten egg

- Pepper to taste

- ½ c water

- 2 c vegetable broth

- 1 tbsp. low-sodium soy sauce

- ¼ tsp red pepper flakes

Let's Cook:

1. Place a large saucepan on the stove over medium heat. Add oil. When oil is hot, add ginger and cook for 1 minute.

2. Add in sherry vinegar, vegetable broth, soy sauce, red pepper flakes and water. Bring this mixture to a boil.

3. Once it is boiling, add seaweed. Gradually add in the egg while stirring.

4. Add scallions and zucchini noodles. Stir in pepper and cook for 2 minutes.

5. Transfer to a bowl and enjoy.

Butternut Squash Soup

Prep Time	20 mins
Cook Time	28 mins
Total Time	48 mins
Servings	8
Calories	125
Carbs	13.2g

Ingredients

- 3 chopped celery ribs

- 6 c low-sodium chicken broth

- ½ chopped white onion

- 1 tsp chopped garlic

- ¼ tsp ground chipotle pepper

- 2 c diced cooked turkey

- 1 tsp chopped cilantro

- ¾ tsp Mexican oregano

- ¾ peeled butternut squash, spiralized

- 2 c diced cooked turkey

Let's Cook:

1. Combine the celery, garlic, onion, chicken broth, oregano, and ground chipotle in a large pot. Place it on the stove over a high heat and bring it to a boil.

2. Cover and reduce heat. Let this simmer until the veggies are soft. This should take about 20 minutes.

3. Stir in the turkey and squash. Simmer the mix until the turkey is heated thoroughly. This should take about 3 to 5 minutes.

4. Garnish with cilantro and enjoy!

Chapter Three: 10 Pastas and Main Dishes

"As long as there's pasta and Chinese food in the world, I'm okay."

-   Michael Chang

In this chapter, I'll help you to:

- Discover how to make a pasta dish without grain

- Create unique and delicious recipes using your spiralizer

Baked Curly Fries

Prep Time	10 mins
Cook Time	20 mins
Total Time	30 mins
Servings	4
Calories	140
Carbs	7g

Ingredients

- 2 washed and dried large white potatoes

- 1 tsp sea salt

- 1 tbsp. evoo

- 2 tbsp. rosemary or thyme

Let's Cook:

1. Preheat your oven to 400 degrees. Put your potatoes through the spiralizer using the blade with the largest triangles.

2. Use a knife or scissors to cut the potato ribbons into smaller bite size fries.

3. Add the potatoes to a bowl and coat them with olive oil.

4. Spread out the fries on two parchment-lined baking sheets. Do not overcrowd on one baking sheet.

5. Sprinkle all the fries with sea salt.

6. Put the trays in your preheated oven and bake them for 15 minutes.

7. Remove them from the oven and flip them over. Remove any fries that are already crispy so they do not burn. Swap the trays before putting them back in the oven. The tray that was on the bottom should be on the top and vice versa.

8. Bake for 10 minutes, checking at 8.

9. Remove the trays, add any additional sea salt to taste and serve.

Extra Tip:

For this recipe, if you want to add fresh herbs, such as rosemary and thyme, sprinkle them over the fries after the first time you took them out of the oven, before you return the trays to the oven the second time.

Seasoned Carrot Noodles

Prep Time	10 mins
Cook Time	5 mins
Total Time	15 mins
Servings	1
Calories	165
Carbs	6.1g

Ingredients

- 1 big spiralized carrot

   Sauce

- 3 tbsp. fresh lemon juice

- 1 tsp grated ginger

- 1 small grated garlic clove

- 1 tbsp. tahini

- 1 tbsp. walnut or olive oil

- 1 tsp tamari

  Garnish

- Parsley

- Sesame seeds

- Pine nuts

Let's Cook:

1. Mix the ingredients for the sauce and stir well.

2. Spiralized your carrot into ribbon noodles.

3. Pour the sauce over the carrots. Mix by hand to coat.

4. Top with garnish.

5. Keeps well in the fridge overnight.

Turkey Bolgonese with Zucchini Noodles

Prep Time	15 mins
Cook Time	15 mins
Total Time	30 mins
Servings	4
Calories	240
Carbs	21.5g

Ingredients

- 1 lb ground turkey

- 1 diced onion

- 2 minced garlic cloves

- 3 tbsp. tomato paste

- 28 ounce can crushed tomatoes

- Salt and pepper

- 2 tablespoons chopped parsley

- 3 zucchinis

- Parmesan Cheese, for garnish

Let's Cook:

1. In a pan or a skillet brown slightly the turkey with vegetables: onions, garlic, tomatoes. Over medium-high heat. Add salt and pepper to taste.

2. Add tomato paste and bring to a simmer. Cook for about 10 minutes, stirring occasionally.

3. Cut zucchini into noodles with your spiralizer.

4. In a large skillet cook the noodles over medium heat. Make sure to not overcook

them. Stir for about 1-2 minutes and they should be done. Add salt and paper.

5. Serve with the turkey Bolognese and sprinkle Parmesan on top.

Pesto Courgetti Noodle Burrata

Prep Time	15 mins
Cook Time	0 mins
Total Time	15 mins
Servings	2-3
Calories	198
Carbs	8.7g

Ingredients

- 3 courgettis
- 5-6 cherry tomatoes
- 1 ball of burrata

- Pesto

- 3 tbsp. of fresh basil

- 1 garlic clove

- ½ c of pine nuts

- ½ c fresh grated parmesan cheese

- 2 tbsp. olive oil

- Salt and pepper to taste

Let's Cook:

1. Spiralize your courgettis.

2. Throw the pesto ingredients together in a blender and puree until you have a green gunge.

3. Toss in pine nuts if you like.

4. Pour spoonfuls of the green mixture over your noodles.

5. Toss by hand, as a spoon will get the noodles tangled together.

6. Pile it all on your serving plate or bowl.

7. Spread tomatoes over the top and unwrap the burrata.

8. Tear up the burrata and drop in crumbles over the courgettis. Drizzle with olive oil. Serve and enjoy!

Bacon Shrimp Scampi

Prep Time	10 mins
Cook Time	15 mins
Total Time	25 mins
Servings	2
Calories	221
Carbs	11g

Ingredients

- 2 pieces of bacon

- 1 pinch of red pepper flakes

- Salt and pepper to taste

- ¼ c minced shallots

- 1 minced garlic clove

- 4 tbsp. lemon juice

- 12 deveined, defrosted shrimps

- 3 medium, peeled zucchinis

- 2 tbsp. chopped parsley

Let's Cook:

1. Put a large skillet on the stove over medium heat. Add bacon and cook for 3 minutes on each side or to your preference. Remove them with a slotted spoon. Transfer to a paper plate or a plate with a paper towel.

2. Leave 1 tbsp. of bacon fat in the skillet. Add garlic and cook for 30 seconds. Add red pepper flakes, shrimp, and shallots. Season with salt and pepper.

3. Let the shrimp cook for 2 minutes. Flip them over and add lemon juice. Cook for two more minutes. Remove the shrimp using a slotted spoon. Set aside.

4. Use the same skillet to cook zucchini noodles. Toss to combine for 2 minutes. Add in shrimp. Crumble in the bacon. Toss this mixture together well. Divide onto two plates. Garnish with parsley.

Extra Tip:

Add 1/4 c of grated Parmesan cheese before you add the shrimp for a bit of extra flavoring.

Spaghetti Puttanesca

Prep Time	2 mins
Cook Time	15 mins
Total Time	17 mins
Servings	2
Calories	180
Carbs	12g

Ingredients

- 1 tbsp. olive oil

- 1 tbsp. capers

- 1 zucchini

- 1 garlic clove

- Pepper and salt to taste

- 1 tsp crushed red pepper

- 1 anchovy fillet

- ¼ c sliced olives

- 1 can of whole peeled tomatoes

Let's Cook:

1. Put a large skillet on the stove over medium heat. Add in olive oil.

2. Add garlic and anchovy when oil is hot. Cook until the anchovy dissolves in the oil.

3. Over the skillet crush up the whole tomatoes with your hands. Pour in about half of the tomato sauce and use a wooden spoon to crush up the remaining chunks. Add 1 tsp of oil from the anchovy tin. Add in the rest of the ingredients.

4. Simmer for 10 to 15 minutes. Liquid from the sauce should be evaporated.

5. Once evaporated, add in zucchini noodles. Cook for 2-3 minutes. Zucchini should be soft. Transfer to serving bowl and enjoy!

Italian Sweet Potato Casserole

Prep Time	30 mins
Cook Time	25 mins
Total Time	55 mins
Servings	4
Calories	98
Carbs	5.1g

Ingredients

- ½ diced onion

- 1 tbsp. basil olive oil

- 1 diced red bell pepper

- 3 minced garlic cloves

- 1 lb. ground turkey

- 1 tsp dried parsley

- 1 tsp dried oregano

- ¼ tsp red pepper flakes

- 14.5 oz. can of diced tomatoes

- 8 oz. sliced fresh mozzarella cheese

- 3 small sweet potatoes

- ½ tsp fennel seeds

- 2 tbsp. fresh chopped basil

Let's Cook:

1. Preheat your oven to 350 degrees.

2. Add olive oil to a large skillet and put it on the stove over medium-high heat.

3. Sauté onion and bell pepper for 3-5 minutes.

4. Add garlic. Sauté for 1-2 minutes.

5. Add in the ground turkey and cook all the way through.

6. Put your fennel seeds, red pepper flakes, oregano, and parsley into a spice grinder.

7. Add ground herbs to your turkey and add the basil and tomatoes. Reduce the heat to low. Simmer for 15 minutes.

8. Cut the ends of the sweet potatoes off. Peel and cut them in half. Spiralize them with Blade C. Add the sweet potatoes to the skillet, toss and cook for 3-5 minutes.

9. Transfer this mixture to an oven-safe dish and put fresh mozzarella cheese on top. Cover them and bake for 15 minutes.

10. Uncover and bake for 5-10 minutes. Cheese should be melted and bubbling.

Extra Tip:

Always wash and peel (if necessary) vegetables before you spiralize them.

Garlic Sweet Potato Noodles

Prep Time	10 mins
Cook Time	15 mins
Total Time	25 mins
Servings	2
Calories	204
Carbs	37g

Ingredients

- 1 tbsp. olive oil

- 4 packed cups of spinach

- ½ c diced white onions

- ½ c cubed pancetta

- 4 large chopped basil leaves

- ¼ c chicken broth

- 1 large peeled sweet potato

- 1 pinch red pepper flakes

- 1 large minced garlic clove

Let's Cook:

1. Put a large skillet on the stove over medium heat. Add in olive oil. When the oil is hot. Add red pepper flakes, garlic, and onions. Cook for 2 minutes. Onions should be translucent.

2. Spiralize your sweet potato into noodles. Add them and the pancetta into the pot and season with pepper and salt to taste. Toss this to combine it and let it cook for 2 minutes.

3. Add in chicken broth and basil. Allow to fully reduce and cook for 3 more minutes. Sweet

potato noodles should be cooked all the way through.

4. Add in baby spinach at the end of cooking. Cook for 2 minutes. Spinach should be wilted.

5. Divide into bowls and serve.

Baked Mexican Chips

Prep Time	15 mins
Cook Time	17 mins
Total Time	32 mins
Servings	6
Calories	59
Carbs	5g

Ingredients

- 2 unpeeled russet potatoes
- Nonfat cooking spray
- 6 bamboo skewers

- 2 tsp taco seasoning mix

- Sea salt to taste

- 2 tsp sriracha sauce

Let's Cook:

1. Preheat your oven to 425 degrees.

2. Use a baking sheet lined with aluminum foil or grease it with cooking spray.

3. Spiralize your potato into long spirals with a straight flat blade on your spiralizer. Cut each one into three.

4. Thread a skewer through the middle of each potato. Push down on it to fan it out. Set skewers on the baking sheet. Spray with cooking spray. Add the taco seasoning on top.

5. Roast in the preheated oven. They should be browned and crispy. This should take about 18 minutes. Season with the sriracha and sea salt.

Zucchini Noodle Primavera

Prep Time	20 mins
Cook Time	14 mins
Total Time	34 mins
Servings	2
Calories	349
Carbs	19g

Ingredients

- 1 zucchini
- ¼ c olive oil
- 1 tsp salt

- 2 tbsp. milk

- 1 c yellow grape tomatoes

- ½ tsp garlic powder

- ½ c grated pecorino cheese

- ½ tsp dried oregano

- ½ tsp ground black pepper

Let's Cook:

1. Cut your zucchini into noodles with your spiralizer. Toss in with salt until well-mixed. Drain on a paper towel. This will take about 20 minutes. Squeeze it to remove all the moisture.

2. Heat up olive oil in a skillet on the stove over medium heat. Add in red bell pepper and onion. Stir frequently and cook until the onion is translucent, , for about 5 minutes.

3. Stir in the tomatoes. Cook for 3 or 4 minutes until they are soft. Stir in the two mixtures and

cook until tender. The mixture should be dry. This should take about 5 minutes.

4. Sprinkle with garlic powder and stir in the milk. This will take about 2 minutes. Add the pepper, oregano, and pecorino cheese. Stir until well mixed. Serve.

Chapter Four: 10 Spiralized Sweet Desserts

"There is no better way to bring people together than with desserts."

- *Gail Simmons*

In this chapter, I'll help you to:

- Make some of the best desserts available

- The delight of spiralized apple desserts

Apple Cranberry Tart

Prep Time	30 mins
Cook Time	38 mins
Total Time	1 hr. 23 mins
Servings	4
Calories	333
Carbs	20g

Ingredients

- ¼ c dried cranberries

- cooking spray

- 2 peeled apples

- 1 tsp lemon juice

- 2 tbsp. white sugar

- ½ tsp vanilla extract

- ½ tsp ground cinnamon

- ¼ tsp salt

- ½ tsp ground nutmeg

- 1 beaten egg white

- 1 tbsp. turbinado sugar

- 1 tbsp. cornstarch

Let's Cook:

1. Put the cranberries in a small bowl. Cover them with boiling water. Let them soak until they are plump. This should take about 15 minutes. Drain.

2. Preheat your oven to 350 degrees. Grease a baking sheet.lightly with cooking spray.

3. Cut the apples with a vertical slice that does not go into the core. Use a straight flat blade to spiralize the apples into thin half slices.

4. Combine the lemon juice, vanilla extract, apples, and cranberries in a mixing bowl and toss to coat well.

5. Mix the cornstarch, nutmeg, cinnamon, salt, and white sugar in a bowl. Stir into the apples.

6. Roll a pie crust out into a 10inch round on a surface that has been coated with flour. Transfer this to a baking sheet.

7. Spoon the apple mixture into the center of this crust. Leave a 2-inch border.

8. Lift up the edge of the crust and fold in the apples. Brush the edge with egg white and sprinkle with the turbinado sugar.

9. Bake for 40 minutes until the apples are tender and the crust is brown.

10. Transfer to a cutting surface and slice into portions.

Extra Tip:

Center your vegetables on the spiralizer whenever you use it. The results are prettier and more likely to come out correctly.

Roasted Vanilla Sweet Potatoes and Apples

Prep Time	20 mins
Cook Time	20 mins
Total Time	40 mins
Servings	4
Calories	278
Carbs	19g

Ingredients

- 1 large peeled, halved sweet potato

- 2 tbsp. brown sugar

- ¼ tsp salt

- 1 pinch ground nutmeg

- 1 pinch ground ginger

- 1.2 tsp ground cinnamon

- 1 large, unpeeled apple

Let's Cook:

1. Preheat oven to 400 degrees. Line a baking sheet with aluminum foil. Spray this with nonstick cooking spray.

2. Split the vanilla bean with the tip of a sharp knife lengthwise. Hold the pod open and scrape out the seeds. Combine vanilla bean, seeds, and olive oil in a small saucepan. Cook over a very low heat for about 5 minutes. The oil should be fragrant. Remove from heat and allow cooling for 5 minutes.

3. Cut the sweet potato and apple into noodles using your spiralizer. Put them in a large mixing bowl.

4. Whisk brown sugar, 2 tbsp. olive oil, salt, nutmeg, cinnamon and ginger in a small bowl until well combined. Drizzle over the sweet potato and apple. Toss well until completely coated.

5. Spread the apple and potato in an even layer on the baking sheet.

6. Bake for 10 minutes until golden. Increase temperature in the oven to 425 and roast until the ends of the sweet potato are brown. This will take about 5 to 10 more minutes.

Spiralized Carrot Pudding

Prep Time	5 mins
Cook Time	20 mins
Total Time	25 mins
Servings	2
Calories	234
Carbs	18g

Ingredients

- 2 c packed spiralized carrots

- 2 tbsp. coconut oil

- 2 tbsp. honey

- ¼ tsp coconut oil

- 2 tsp and 1 tsp cinnamon

Let's Cook:

1. Put the carrots you have spiralized into a skillet with ¼ tsp of coconut oil. Sauté this for 5 minutes.

2. While they are cooking, put the remaining coconut oil, 2 tsp of cinnamon and the honey into a pot.

3. Put the pot over low heat and stir frequently. All the ingredients should be melted and the sauce will form after five minutes. Keep the heat low and stir constantly.

4. Remove the sauce from the stove and add it to the carrots. Return the mixture back to the stove and turn it on to medium heat for 15 minutes.

5. Test it. The carrots should be soft and creamy.

6. Serve while warm.

Persimmon Pudding

Prep Time	15 mins
Cook Time	0 mins
Total Time	15 mins
Servings	1
Calories	92
Carbs	5g

Ingredients

- 1 Pomegranate
- 1 tbsp. Chia seeds
- ½ tsp vanilla extract

- 1 mashed ripe banana

- 6 tbsp. water

Let's Cook:

1. Put the water and chia seeds into a medium sized bowl and let it sit for 10 minutes.

2. Peel the pomegranate. Remove the seeds.

3. Spiralize the persimmon.

4. Layer in a cup or bowl with the soft ingredients on the bottom of the hard ingredients on top.

5. Serve and enjoy.

Apple Spaghetti with Cinnamon

Prep Time	10 mins
Cook Time	0 mins
Total Time	10 mins
Servings	2
Calories	257
Carbs	10g

Ingredients

- 2 tsp honey

- 1 small container of plain Greek yogurt

- 2 tsp honey

- ¼ tsp vanilla extract

- ¼ tsp ground cinnamon

- ¼ c chopped walnuts

Let's Cook:

1. Attach the apple to a spiralizer and cut it into ribbons.

2. Whisk cinnamon, vanilla extract, honey, and Greek yogurt in a mixing bowl until blended. Add the apple and toss it to coat.

3. Garnish with walnuts.

Extra Tip:

Buy a special brush to clean your spiralizer and keep it clean.

Cinnamon Sugar Apple Noodles

Prep Time	10 mins
Cook Time	8 mins
Total Time	18 mins
Servings	2
Calories	65
Carbs	4.6g

Ingredients

- 1 apple

- 2 tbsp. butter

- 2 tbsp. sugar

- 2 tsp cinnamon

Let's Cook:

1. Using a spiralizer, make long noodles out of the apple.

2. Heat the butter in a small pan until it is foaming.

3. Add the apples and sauté them for 3 minutes. They should be soft.

4. Add cinnamon and sugar. Stir well until it is well mixed.

5. Continue to cook for another 5 minutes until they are soft.

6. Put the mix on ice cream or in a pie.

7. Enjoy!

Spiralized Apple Crumbs

Prep Time	10 mins
Cook Time	0 mins
Total Time	10 mins
Servings	8
Calories	107
Carbs	8.7g

Ingredients

- 1 tsp cinnamon

- 1/3 c coconut sugar

- 9 medium red apples

- ½ of an orange (just the juice)

- Zest of one orange

  Crumble

- 1 c rolled oats

- 1 c almond meal

- 1 tsp cinnamon

- ¼ c coconut oil

- 1/3 c coconut sugar

- Pinch of salt

- Pinch of nutmeg

Let's Cook:

1. Preheat the oven to 350 degrees. Spray down a 9x13 inch baking dish with the coconut oil spray.

2. Spiralize the apples with the largest setting. Put them in a big bowl and top them with

coconut sugar, cinnamon, orange juice, and zest.

3. Spread out in a baking dish.

4. Add the rolled oats, almond meal, cinnamon, nutmeg, salt, and coconut sugar in a large bowl. Stir frequently. Place coconut oil in a bowl and use your hands to mix it together until crumbly. Don't be shy. Mix it well.

5. Sprinkle crumble mixture on top of apples.

6. Bake this for 40 minutes and take it out. Serve it warm.

Sweet Potato with Whipped Maple Ricotta

Prep Time	25 mins
Cook Time	45 mins
Total Time	1 hour 10 mins
Servings	2-3
Calories	203
Carbs	15.2g

Ingredients

- 1 c whole milk ricotta

- 1 gluten-free pie crust

- Pinch of salt

- 2 tbsp. maple syrup

- 1 ½ large purple sweet potatoes

- 1 ½ large orange sweet potatoes

- ¼ c olive oil

- 1 tsp cinnamon

- Salt and pepper to taste

Let's Cook:

1. Prepare the gluten-free pie crust, based on your dietary needs. Chill the dough for 30 minutes in the refrigerator.

2. During this time, trim the sweet potatoes and spiralize them. Cut them into long, skinny ribbons.

3. Preheat the oven to 350 degrees. Grease a tart pan. Roll the dough on a floured surface so that it is just a bit bigger than your tart tin. Transfer

the dough to the pan and press down on the bottoms and sides.

4. Trim the excess from the edges and refrigerate for 15 minutes.

5. Line the dough with parchment paper. Fill with a pie weight. Bake for 15 minutes. The edges should be golden brown.

6. Take this from the oven and set aside so that it will cool off.

7. Make the whipped maple ricotta by combining the syrup, ricotta, and salt in a blender. The ricotta should be smooth and fluffy.

8. Spread the maple ricotta on the bottom of the tart. Quickly dip one sweet potato slice in the olive oil. You can also use a pastry brush to cover more of them easily.

9. Roll the strip into a tight circle. Place it in the middle of the tart. Dip the next one in olive oil and roll it around the first slice. Continue wrapping the slices in a circle until the tart is full.

10.   Brush the top with what's left of the olive oil and sprinkle with salt, pepper, and cinnamon.

11. Bake the tart at 350 degrees for 45 minutes. The sweet potatoes should be soft. Cool in the pan for 40 minutes, slice and serve it up with your favorite healthy toppings.

Extra Tip:

You will find that your spiralizer will make one long noodle. To avoid jamming in the spiralizer, be sure to frequently cut the noodles into smaller pieces.

Spiralized Apple Tartlets

Prep Time	15 mins
Cook Time	0 mins
Total Time	15 mins
Servings	3
Calories	187
Carbs	9.2g

Ingredients

- ½ c pitted dates
- ½ tsp cinnamon
- 1 c dried apple slices

- Filling

- 1 spiralized apple

- ½ tsp cinnamon

- 2 tbsp. coconut sugar

Let's Cook:

1. Spiralize the apples until they are cut into small ribbons. Add dates and cinnamon in a food processor or blender until a ball is formed. Press this dough and the apples into 3 tart pans or muffin tins lined with plastic wrap. We suggest you keep some of the apple ribbons for garnish.

2. Refrigerate.

3. Sprinkle the apple noodles with the coconut sugar and cinnamon.

4. Refrigerate overnight.

5. The next day, assemble and enjoy!

Baked Spiral Apple Chips

Prep Time	10 mins
Cook Time	2 hours
Total Time	2 hours 10 mins
Servings	3
Calories	105
Carbs	6.7g

Ingredients

- 2 apples

- 1 tsp ground cinnamon

- 2 tsp granulated sugar

Let's Cook:

1. Preheat your oven to 250 degrees. Line a baking sheet with parchment paper. Set aside.

2. Run the apples through the spiralizer. Cut down into one-half of the apples using a paring knife to separate the slices into rings. Place these slices into a bowl.

3. Combine cinnamon and sugar together in a small mixing bowl. Sprinkle this mixture over the spiralized apple slices. Toss them slightly to make sure they are completely covered.

4. Place these slices in a single layer on the baking sheet.

5. Bake for an hour. Flip each apple slice over and bake for another hour. Shut off the oven and let the apple chips sit until they are mostly cooled. This will make them crispy.

6. Store leftovers in an airtight container for up to three days.

Best Practices & Common Mistakes

Do's

Remove Noodles from Water

Keep in mind that the longer you keep noodles in the water, whether they are zucchini or any other type of noodle, water will seep out. Your sauce will be watery if you are not careful.

Keep your Spiralizer Clean

Use one particular sponge and brush for your spiralizer and clean it after every use. Store it after cleaning. Never store it dirty with food remnants stuck to it.

Dry Your Noodles

As mentioned previously, noodles will expel water. Before using them, always dry them on a paper towel and squeeze out the excess water (especially from zucchini noodles) before using them.

Don'ts

Cook the Noodles Every Time

You will find that sometimes you do not need to cook spiralized vegetable noodles. If the recipe does not call for cooking, you can feel safe that spiralizing the noodles, dressing them and eating them is a great option.

Stray from Your Diet Plan

As tempting as it might be for some people, recipes that call for ingredients that are not in your diet plan should be avoided. Go online and search for a substitution. There is nearly always an ingredient that can be switched out with another to avoid allergic reactions or simply because you don't like the taste.

Leftovers

Make sure you are storing your leftovers according to the ingredients. Meals made with apples should always be refrigerated and not kept for more than a few days unless they have been dried or the recipe says they are good for longer.

Conclusion

Knowing the basics of using your spiralizer will make using one a lot easier. Spiralizers can be purchased at most department stores and come in a variety of brand names. They are typically adjustable so that you can use different blades for different sizes of noodles. You can even get a handheld spiralizer. This is good for someone who lives alone and is only cooking for themselves. Restaurant chefs use large spiralizers to create beautiful plates.

This book has thirty recipes for you to try. You can adjust the ingredients to make more or less, depending on your needs. If you are used to cooking for a family, you will probably be able to adjust the ingredients without a problem. If you are unsure, it is always best to consult online resources to make sure you are doing it right.

One of the tips we don't want you to forget is to wash the vegetables or fruits before you put them through the spiralizer. This goes along with cleaning your spiralizer and making sure it is not stored with food remnants stuck to the blades or any other part of the appliance.

You'll quickly learn how easy it is to use a spiralizer and how pretty your meals will turn out to be, not to mention tasty and delicious. For someone on a gluten-free, grain-free, low carb diet, the spiralizer is a must have. Replacing regular, traditional noodles with those of a healthier variety will keep you sticking to your diet plan. It is best to check the package on your ingredients to make sure you have chosen the gluten-free or grain-free variety.

We hope you enjoy these recipes. We have tried to provide you with the best available on the Internet today. Try each of them and pick out your favorites. Adjust as needed. Most of all, enjoy!!

Bonus: Your FREE Gift

As a token of our appreciation, please take advantage of the **FREE Gift** - a lifetime **VIP Membership** at our book club.

Follow the link below to download your FREE books:

http://bit.ly/vipbookclub

As a VIP member, you will get an instant **FREE** access to exclusive new releases and bestselling books.